W9-CDM-911

WITHDRAWN

EXCAVATING THE PAST

DINOSAUR DIGS

Mary Quigley

Heinemann Library
Chicago, Illinois

© 2006 Heinemann Library
a division of Reed Elsevier Inc.
Chicago, Illinois

Customer Service 888–454–2279

Visit our website at
www.heinemannraintree.com

All rights reserved. No part of this publication
may be reproduced, or transmitted in any form
or by any means, electronic, mechanical,
including photocopying, recording, taping, or
any information storage and retrieval system,
without permission in writing from the
publishers.

Photo research by Maria Joannou and Catherine
Bevan
Designed by Richard Parker and Tinstar Design
Ltd (www.tinstar.co.uk)
Printed in China by WKT Company Limited

10 09 08 07 06
10 9 8 7 6 5 4 3 2 1

**Library of Congress Cataloging-in-
Publication Data**

Quigley, Mary, 1963-
    Dinosaur digs / Mary Quigley.
        p. cm. -- (Excavating the past)
    Includes bibliographical references and
index.
    ISBN 1-4034-5996-7 (library binding -
hardcover)
    1. Dinosaurs--Juvenile literature. 2.
Paleontology--Juvenile literature. I. Title. II.
Series.
    QE861.5.Q85 2006
    567.9--dc22

2005009180

Acknowledgments
The publishers would like to thank the following
for permission to reproduce photographs: Alamy
pp. 18, 22 (Phil Degginger/Carnegie Museum), 42
(BananaStock); Associated Press pp. 39 (David
Duprey), 43 (Al Grillo); Corbis pp. 12 (Sygma/ Vo
Trung Dung), 13 (Sygma/ Vo Trung Dung); Corbis
pp. 9 (Bettmann), 10 (Bettmann), 19 (Dave G.
Houser), 21 (Louie Psihoyos), 23 (Reuters), 24, 27,
29 (Louie Psihoyos), 34 (Tom Bean), 36 (Danny
Lehman), 37, (Gary Braasch); Geoscience Features
pp. 8, 17, 2, 31; Natural History Museum pp. 6, 7,
8, 14, 15, 26, 30, 32; Rich McCrea pp. 11, 35,
38; Royal Tyrell Museum of Paleontology,
Canada p. 20; Science Photo Library/ D. Van
Ravensway p. 41.

Cover photograph of dinosaur tracks reproduced
with permission of Corbis (Danny Lehman.) Small
photograph of a dinosaur skeleton reproduced with
permission of the Natural History Museum.

The author would like to thank Dr. Scott D.
Sampson and Professor James Farlow for their help
with the research for this book.

The publishers would like to thank Peter
Makovicky, of the Field Museum of Natural History
in Chicago, Illinois, for his assistance in the
preparation of this book.

Illustrations by Jeff Edwards and Eikon Illustration

Every effort has been made to contact
copyright holders of any material reproduced in
this book. Any omissions will be rectified in
subsequent printings if notice is given to the
publishers.

CONTENTS

INTRODUCTION

Millions of years ago dinosaurs roamed Earth. They lived among turtles, lizards, frogs, early mammals, alligators, and crocodiles, but humans did not yet exist. Dinosaurs were reptiles. The name "dinosaur" has come to mean "terrible lizard." The name was chosen by Richard Owen, an early paleontologist, who was so fascinated with dinosaurs that he had life-size models of them created.

Being called a terrible lizard makes dinosaurs sound fierce and frightening, and some of them were. Meat eaters, called carnivores, prowled the land looking for food. They relied on speed, strength, and special features, such as sharp claws, to guarantee a meal. Not all dinosaurs were carnivores. Many were herbivores, who fed on plants.

▷ *The ground shook when gentle giants, like this* **diplodocus,** *wandered in search of food.*

Three periods

Dinosaurs lived in a time called the Mesozoic Era. It is divided into three time periods called Triassic, Jurassic, and Cretaceous. About 245 million to 208 million years ago, in the Triassic Period, the first dinosaurs appeared. At that time all the continents were grouped together in a huge land mass that we call Pangaea, meaning "all earth."

The Triassic period

During the Triassic period, the areas around the edges of Pangaea were wet and full of plant life. In the central region were dry deserts. The oceans (Panthalassa) were filled with reptiles, such as nothosaurs and placodonts. There were some familiar creatures, however, such as insects, spiders, and crocodiles. Early ancestors of frogs and toads lived in the Triassic period.

Many Triassic dinosaurs were herbivores. The plants that were available were hard to digest, so early herbivores developed huge stomachs that could break down the bulky food. They also swallowed small stones that helped break down the food.

▷ *Land masses on Earth's surface have moved over time, so they have not always looked as they do today.*

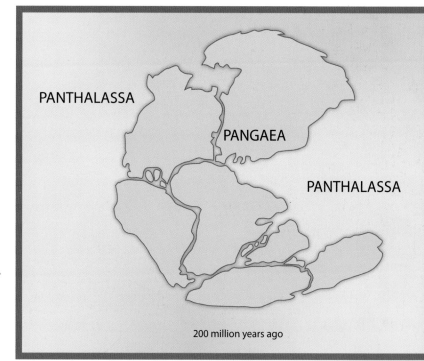

PANTHALASSA

PANGAEA

PANTHALASSA

200 million years ago

The Jurassic period

During the Jurassic period, 208 million to 146 million years ago, Earth was different from in the Triassic period. Pangaea broke apart into two large land masses that we call Laurasia and Gondwanaland. The dinosaurs on each of the two land masses were now separated by oceans and they developed in separate, unique ways. The climate was very warm and moist. Plant types that had existed for millions of years thrived and new kinds of plants were developing. This was great news for the herbivores, who found more to eat.

The carnivorous dinosaurs thrived, too, with plenty of animals to hunt. As animals settled into particular habitats, or living areas, they developed a variety of features and habits that helped them to survive. Small mammals, flying reptiles, and marine reptiles, which had appeared in the Triassic period, still survived. There were only a few small mammals. They developed fur coats as a way to adjust to their living conditions.

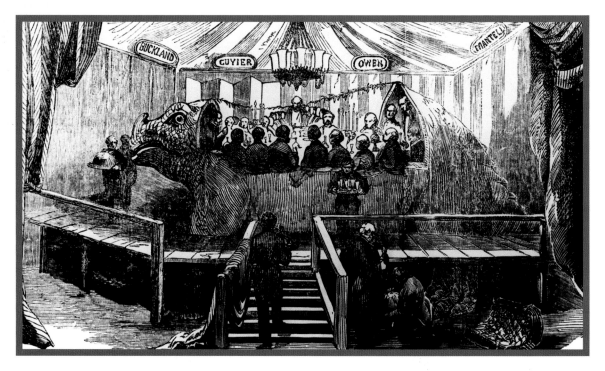

△ *Richard Owen's* Iguanodon *replica was so large that he invited people to a dinner party inside of it!*

The Cretaceous period

The last period of the Mesozoic Era, the Cretaceous period, was 146 million to 65 million years ago. By this time the surface of Earth had moved to create the continents as they look today. Climates changed, too. In the face of such dramatic changes, plant and animal life responded by continuing to adapt. Some plants survived, despite the appetites of herbivores, by producing flowers as a part of their design for fast reproduction. The plants and animals that did not adapt did not survive.

During this period, dinosaurs lived all around the world. But, by the end of the Cretaceous, all the dinosaurs were extinct. These creatures who lived millions of years before man still interest us. We can discover their story through fossils.

Paleontology Challenge

Fossils are an excellent record of animals and plants, but they can be misleading. Only under rare conditions will feathers, fur, or fine leaves stay intact long enough to be preserved in stone. This means that when paleontologists study fossils they cannot always tell whether an animal had fur. They cannot say for certain that there were no grasses in a certain region just because they have not yet found proof of them. Some climate conditions and land formations are more likely to produce fossils, but the absence of fossils in certain places does not mean that there were no dinosaurs there.

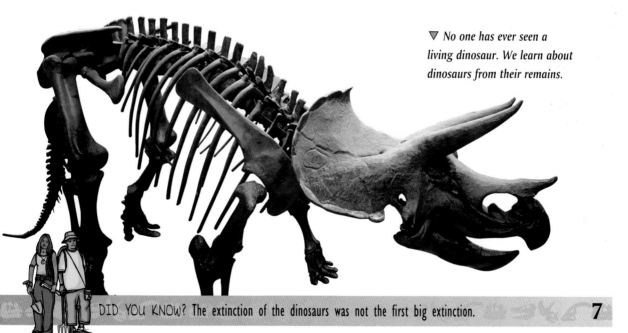

▽ *No one has ever seen a living dinosaur. We learn about dinosaurs from their remains.*

THE BASICS OF PALEONTOLOGY

How can we know so much about creatures that lived millions of years before people did? It is all thanks to the work of thousands of scientists over hundreds of years. Paleontologists are scientists who study prehistoric life. They are like detectives looking for clues, and the clues they try to find are fossils. Fossils are prints, casts, or hardened remains in stone, which can teach us a lot about dinosaurs. Fossils may be of bones, teeth, skin, feathers, eggs, tracks, nests, or even body waste. Paleontologists study dinosaurs to understand the story of life on Earth better.

Fantasy or Fact?

There are references to "dragon bones" in Chinese writings from around C.E. 265 Were these "dragon bones" actually the fossils of dinosaurs? Some people believed they had magical properties and ground them into medicine. Fossils were also sometimes turned into tools or jewelry.

Early fossil finds

Imagine how puzzling dinosaur fossils would have been to people who discovered them before paleontology, when we had not yet figured out that such creatures had existed. Some dinosaur egg shells were found at a dig in the Gobi Desert in 1925 by Roy Chapman Andrews and a group from the American Museum of Natural History. But someone had found them before Andrews' group did. They had been worked into various shapes by ancient humans. In Brazil very old carvings made by people have been found right alongside fossilized dinosaur tracks.

◀▶ Fossils vary from huge thigh bones (right) to eggs (left) that never hatched.

WHO WAS George Cuvier?

George Cuvier was a French scientist who lived from 1769 to 1832. He studied anatomy and believed that all the organs and features of the body worked together. He also started the idea of extinction, by suggesting that it was possible for certain species to die out completely. He used his interest in anatomy to further the science of paleontology. Some people call him the "Father of Paleontology."

Surely the same people who had made the carvings had seen the tracks that had been made ages before. But who did they think made them? Native people of Canada referred to fossils as being the remains of "the grandfather of the buffalo," according to Jean L'Heureux. He was a French-Canadian traveler who lived among the Piegan people of Alberta in the early 1900s.

When earlier people stumbled across fossils, they often believed that the bones belonged to creatures that they knew, or that were part of their myths or religion. Sometimes they thought the fossils were from dragons or saints. Long ago, when many areas of Earth were still unexplored, people thought that fearsome creatures could be hidden in the thick jungles or deep out in the oceans. This made travelers both curious and fearful.

Fantasy or Fact?

In 1676 Robert Plot, a museum curator in Oxfordshire, England, was sent a bone that he first thought was from an elephant. Later he wondered if it was from a giant. In 1763 naturalist Richard Brookes agreed that it was from a giant. The bone was lost, but drawings of it, and the studies of William Buckland, suggested that it was really the bone of a Megalosaurus.

◁ *Leonardo Da Vinci drew sketches of fossils that he found.*

Later discoveries

Dr. Casper Wistar and
Matlack Wistar found the first
documented United States fossil
of a dinosaur in 1787. Discoveries were
not as well catalogued in the early days of the
science as they are now, so little more is known about their find.
Some have suggested that the fossil was part of a hadrosaur. The
Wistars' discovery increased people's fascination with dinosaurs.
Sometimes people got so excited about dinosaurs that news reports
about them were heavily exaggerated. There was strong competition
among dinosaur hunters to find the best fossils.

EYEWITNESS

"Most Colossal Animal Ever on Earth
Just Found Out West. When it walked the Earth
trembled under its weight of 120,000 pounds
(54 tons), when it ate it filled a stomach big enough to
hold 3 elephants, when it was angry its roar could be
heard 10 miles away, and when it stood up its height
was equal to 11 stories of a sky-scraper."

New York Herald, 1898 description of the dinosaur after William Reed
discovered its large fossilized thigh bone in Utah.

▽ *Paleontologists
may have to work in
blistering sun or bitter
cold to find new fossils.
In the past they only
had very basic tools.*

Fantasy or Fact?

Even today people still make claims of seeing unusual animals, such as the Loch Ness Monster in Scotland. Those who believe they have seen it, describe a creature that resembles a plesiosaur, a marine animal that lived at the same time as dinosaurs. Whether the Loch Ness Monster exists or not is uncertain. But it is definite that people are fascinated by unusual creatures and the possibility of meeting one face to face.

The work of a paleontologist

Although scientific techniques have changed a lot since the days of the Wistars, the excitement about dinosaurs is the same. It has helped to support the work of paleontologists, who try to unearth more about the lives of dinosaurs. Luckily there is always more to learn about dinosaurs, and plenty of opportunities for those who study them to make new and amazing discoveries.

▽ *Paleontologists now use very advanced equipment to help them find and excavate fossils.*

Finding fossils

Paleontologists must be skilled at knowing where to look for fossils. Paleontologists begin by finding a location for their dig. A dig is an excavation of earth or rock made in order to search for artifacts, fossils, or other things that tell us about the history of life on Earth. A paleontologist might choose a spot for a dig because other fossils have been found near by.

Sometimes the paleontologist will take a chance on a new location, but not at random. It is important to know a lot about the geologic history of Earth. Certain land forms, types of rock, or climates favor the preservation of fossils. Also by knowing the history of volcanic eruptions or other natural force, a paleontologist can make a very educated guess about where to begin. Often they will choose a spot where rock is exposed, such as a cliff.

Paleontology Challenge

When Gideon Mantell found bones of an *Iguanodon*, he thought one bone looked like a horn, so he placed it on the nose of the dinosaur. Later Louis Dollo realized that it was actually a thumb spike, based on what he learned from newly discovered skeletons in a Belgian coal mine. His reconstructed *Iguanodon* had the spikes on the thumbs, but was posed incorrectly in an upright stance. It was not until the 1970s that *Iguanodon* was understood to be a dinosaur that walked on all fours. Each newly found fossil and the creative thinking of each of the paleontologists furthered the understanding of dinosaur anatomy.

▷ *Paleontologists must carry out surveys of the land before deciding where to dig.*

Although paleontologists search deliberately to find fossils, sometimes using satellites or sonar, there are still many times when fossils are found by chance, when someone is excavating for a new road, or plowing a field. Sometimes, spring thaws cause water to trickle along cliffs, revealing new layers of dinosaur history. As land shifts, rocks, dirt, and fossils can be heaved up into plain view. A hiker might be setting up camp and then notice that there is more than ordinary rock underfoot. They may have found a jawbone or a skeleton.

Excavating fossils

After finding a fossil, paleontologists work carefully and slowly, clearing away stone, dirt, and sand. This takes patience because they have to get the fossil out without damaging it. Some digging is done with shovels, but as the workers get nearer to the fossil they may switch to brushes that let them work gently. Other equipment includes goggles to protect their eyes from debris and magnifying glasses to study what they are uncovering. It can take many years to dig up the fossils from just one dinosaur. Paleontologists use photographs and drawings to document the fossils as they find them so that reconstruction can be more accurate. They may use CAT scans or laser scans to obtain a precise image of the fossil that can be used in producing a copy of it for study or display.

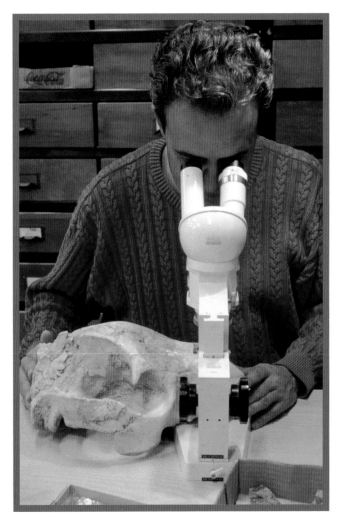

△ *Microscopes reveal information that cannot be seen with the naked eye.*

TYPES OF DINOSAURS

Hundreds of different species of dinosaurs have been identified so far, and it is very likely that many are yet to be discovered. The variety is a result of them developing in unique ways to survive in their surroundings—fossils have been found all over the world.

Dinosaur groupings

Scientists divide dinosaurs into two main groups. Saurischian dinosaurs have hips like lizards and ornithischian dinosaurs have hips like birds. Saurischian dinosaurs tend to have longer necks and grasping hands. Dinosaurs in the Saurischia group include both carnivores and herbivores. All the dinosaurs discovered so far in the Ornithischia group are herbivores.

The sauropods belonged to the Saurischia group. They measured from 23 feet (7 meters) to over 133 feet (40 meters) long. They were herbivores with extremely long necks and tails.

◁ *Sometimes complete skeletons are found. They show us just how big some dinosaurs were.*

△ *Carnivorous dinosaurs, like this one, had teeth for tearing meat.*

Their size and the need to protect their herd explains why sauropods were slow. Their heavy bodies and plodding gait could not win them any races. Sauropods first appear in the Jurassic. This was perfect timing because they thrived on the increasingly lush vegetation. They had a huge appetite to support their amazing growth, eating nearly constantly in order to gain a ton a year, or more.

Paleontology Challenge

Even with fossils in hand, paleontologists have to work very hard to develop a complete and accurate representation of how each dinosaur looked and lived. For instance fossils have shown that sauropods had very long necks. But how do paleontologists figure out whether they used their necks to dine on leaves up high in the trees? In fact how could they even lift such an immense neck? Paleontologists get help from medical scientists, who can use CAT scans to reveal that the neck bones of sauropods are porous and light, like the bones of birds. That means their necks were light enough for them to lift.

▷ Diplodocus *was a type of sauropod. It was huge, but its brain was tiny.*

Theropods

Theropods were another group of saurischian dinosaurs, who were smaller than the sauropods. The theropods were all carnivores. They had large heads and mouths, sharp, blade-like serrated teeth up to 7 inches (17.5 centimeters) long, and powerful hind legs.

These dinosaurs were built to be hunters. Theropods were swift and able to run as fast as 25 miles (40 kilometers) per hour. They had light, hollow bones, which helped them to maintain speed. They had three or fewer fingers on each hand. One type of theropod, *Spinosaurus*, had an unusual sail on its back, which may have released body heat in its warm habitat. *Megalosaurus* is another example of a theropod.

Ceratopsians

The ornithischians appear to all have been herbivores. They include the horned dinosaurs called ceratopsians. *Triceratops* was the first horned dinosaur to be discovered, in 1888. It is also one of the best known. It is named for its three facial horns. It also had a horned beak and neck frills.

◄ Tyrannosaurus rex *is perhaps the best known of all carnivores and has been called the "king of dinosaurs." It belongs to the theropod group.*

Hadrosaurs

Some ornithischians developed a snout that was shaped rather like the bill of a duck. They are called hadrosaurs. *Maiasaura* is one kind of hadrosaur. The name means "good mother lizard." Fossils of *Maiasaura* nests and eggs have inspired scientists to study the nurturing aspects of dinosaur parents. *Corythosaurus*, another hadrosaur, has a crest on its head that looks like the top of a helmet.

Iguanodons

Iguanodons belong to a group of ornithischian dinosaurs called iguanodontids. The name *Iguanodon* means "iguana tooth." *Hypsilophodons* had a beak like a turtle to nip leaves from plants. The hypsilophodon group also included the small *Leaellynasaurus*, who lived in the polar region on land that would later drift and be called Australia.

Other ornithischians

Armored *Ankylosaurs* and spiny, plated *Stegosaurs* added yet more variety to the ornisthiscian group of dinosaurs. *Stegosaurs* are known for the dorsal plates that run down their back. Some types had large spines on their tail that could be used in defense. Though they were herbivores, they were still very dangerous animals. *Edmontonia* is one example of an ankylosaur.

△ *The Hadrosaur's duck-like bill is evident from its skeleton.*

Paleontology Challenge

Even though ornithischian means "bird-hipped," scientists think that birds are actually descended from the lizard-hipped saurischians. There are many other similarities between theropods and birds, including hollow bones and bipedel (two-footed) running. Birds, such as ostriches, have striking similarity to some theropods.

FOSSIL EVIDENCE

Fossils are remarkable because most plants and animals do not leave a permanent record of their appearance. In nature plants that die are eaten or rot away.

Fossils exist because of dramatic acts of nature. A volcano eruption may trap plants and animals in lava or ash. The resin of trees traps insects. A tar pit or quick sand also can be a future fossil site. Stagnant or toxic water can prevent the usual breakdown of tissue. When the bones themselves remain, it is because the bones were the hardest part of the animal, made of the mineral calcium.

EYEWITNESS

"Since things are much more ancient than letters, it is no marvel if, in our day, no records exist of these seas having covered so many countries . . . But sufficient for us is the testimony of things created in the salt waters, and found again in high mountains far from the seas."

Leonardo Da Vinci

▷ *This cliff and riverbed are prime locations for the discovery of fossils.*

WHO WAS Leonardo Da Vinci?

Leonardo Da Vinci was born in Italy in 1452. He was a naturalist, artist, and engineer, who carefully observed the world around him. Fossils of shells up on mountain tops where there was no sea intrigued him. He figured out that the ocean must have been higher in the past, covering those mountains and leaving behind clams that made fossils over time. He was way ahead of many people of his time in his understanding of the natural history of Earth.

WHO WAS Johann Beringer?

Johann Beringer was a scientist. In the 1720s he uncovered rocks covered with the design of grapes and a squid-like creature. Thinking he had found real fossils, he published his discovery. He was embarrassed when he discovered that someone had created fake fossils.

△ *This dinosaur bone has been petrified.*

Paleontology Challenge

Fossils are not always what they appear to be. Some rocks naturally form shapes that look like an arm or a head. They may have patterns that look like ferns, but this is caused by the composition of the rock. Sometimes people have actually created fake fossils, just for the publicity. Sometimes real finds can be wrongly identified. Long ago the horn of the narwhal was thought to belong to the mythical creature, the unicorn.

Preservation

When someone finds a fossil, it is evidence that something extraordinary has happened. An animal or plant has been caught in a rare situation that preserved its form. Millions of years later, a paleontologist might find fossils of the dinosaur. Perhaps it will be a print in the stone, all that is left after all those years. Or maybe other minerals have seeped into the bones of the dinosaur, creating a nearly perfect cast of the skeleton. When a stone replica of a plant or animal is made in this way, we say it is petrified.

Learning from fossils

What can we learn from fossils? A 4-foot (1.2- meter) rib bone gives us an idea of how huge one dinosaur might be overall. Teeth can be studied to know whether the dinosaur ate meat or plants. The design of hips and legs can help us to know how fast dinosaurs walked. We can learn whether they walked on all four legs or upright on just two. We can tell if they carried their weight on their toes or on wide, flat feet. Porous bones indicate a lightweight skeleton, and feathers show a connection between dinosaurs and the birds of today.

Paleontology Challenge

For many years paleontologists wondered if dinosaurs were warm-blooded animals, who produced their own body heat, or cold-blooded animals, who depended on their heat from external sources, such as sunlight. One scientist found growth rings, like trees have, in some dinosaur bones. This is typical of cold-blooded animals that have seasonal growth spurts. Since our modern reptiles are cold-blooded, this seems like a reasonable way of life for dinosaurs as well.

Just as bone structure seemed to prove the case for cold-blooded dinosaurs, some bones also show evidence of rapid growth, which is more typical of warm-blooded animals. Since warm-blooded birds are thought to be the descendants of dinosaurs, the evidence can seem to favor this argument as well. Today many paleontologists think that dinosaurs may have had some features of each.

◁ *The horns and frill on the fossilized skull of a* Triceratops *give us clues about how it defended itself.*

Learning about behavior

Some fossils can show us dinosaur behavior. In Mongolia a *Velociraptor* and *Protoceratops* were locked in combat, millions of years ago. Neither won the battle. Their fossilized skeletons were found entwined with a claw of the *Velociraptor* in the stomach region of the *Protoceratops*. The *Protoceratops* had its jaws clamped around an arm of the *Velociraptor*. Before either could win, an act of nature, probably a collapsing sand dune or a massive sandstorm, killed them both and preserved the evidence.

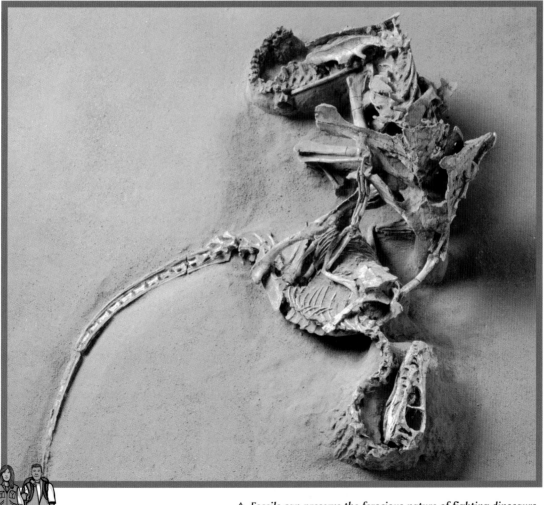

△ *Fossils can preserve the ferocious nature of fighting dinosaurs.*

Other clues

Fossils give us an idea of the sounds dinosaurs might have produced. By looking at the shape of the skull and nasal passages, scientists can figure out what sounds were possible. They can even blow air through models of these passages to try to recreate the sounds that the dinosaurs made.

Sometimes a print of skin texture is found at a fossil site. Though the skin itself is gone, the print lets us know if the skin was bumpy, smooth, or even feathered.

Dinosaur National Monument

Dinosaur National Monument, located in Utah and Colorado, gives a unique presentation of fossils. A variety of about 1,600 dinosaur bones are cemented in a stone wall collage. This natural formation is like a timeline that chronicles dinosaur history. A *Camarasaurus* skull and neck protrude from the stone, in a lifelike pose. Paleontologists decided to leave the fossils in the stone, so people can come and see them there as they were placed long ago by an act of nature.

WHO IS Sue Hendrickson?

Born in Chicago, Illinois in 1949, Sue Hendrickson had been a field paleontologist since the mid 1980s. In 1990, she was traveling with a team of fossil hunters from the Black Hills Institute. They needed repairs on tires for their truck and went into town, except for Sue who chose to stay behind to keep looking for fossils. She found some crumbled rock and looked up to find dinosaur bones in the rocks above. It turned out that she had discovered the largest and most complete skeleton of a Tyrannosaurus rex. The detail on the bones is so refined that it is possible to see where muscles and tendons attached to bone. The Tyrannosaurus rex was named "Sue" after her, even though we do not know whether it was male or female. This Tyrannosaurus rex is now housed in the Field Museum, in Chicago, Illinois.

What can we learn from Tyrannosaurus Sue?

The huge teeth are shaped for piercing and grabbing, so we can assume that a *Tyrannosaurus rex* preferred a diet of meat and was a predator. This seems to be confirmed by the skull having eye sockets for forward facing eyes. This is a feature of many predatory animals, as it means they can judge distances well. On prey animals the eyes are often set to the sides offering a wider view of predators. The design of the brain cavity shows a particularly well developed area for interpreting smells—useful for sniffing out hidden meals.

DID YOU KNOW? Dinosaur fossils are often crushed or misshapen by Earth's movement.

WHO IS John "Jack" Horner?

Jack Horner is a very famous paleontologist, who discovered and named two species of dinosaurs, Maiasaura and Orodromeus. He was born in 1946 in Montana and he was the technical advisor for Steven Spielberg's Jurassic Park movies. In 1978 he discovered the first nest of baby dinosaurs recorded in the world, and the next year he discovered the first fossil dinosaur eggs ever discovered and recorded in the Western hemisphere. His finds were significant because they opened up a new area of study, which focused on nesting and parenting. He found several preserved embryos.

Coprolites

Dinosaurs did not just leave behind their bones, but also their body waste. Fossilized solid body waste is called coprolite. At first some people think this is a strange way to study dinosaurs. But some really interesting things can be learned from coprolites. They tell paleontologists about the variety of foods that dinosaurs ate. There is one problem. It is hard to know which dinosaur left which coprolite. Occasionally a lucky paleontologist finds a coprolite still with the animal that produced it. Fossilized stomach contents are sometimes more useful because they are found with the rest of the dinosaur. That makes it easier to know exactly what was on each dinosaur's menu.

EYEWITNESS

"Dino Dung: Paleontology's Next Frontier? Items found in dinosaur and other ancient animal coprolites include fossilized bone, teeth, fur, plant stems, seeds, pollen, wood chips, fungus, insects, larvae, dung beetle burrows, fish scales, shells, and glassy marine organism microfossils 30 to 50 microns [1 to 2 thousandths of an inch] in size, among others."

Sean Markey, National Geographic News, March 12, 2003

Fantasy or Fact?

When paleontologists discovered small, fossilized animals in the stomach area of a fossilized *Coelophysis* they were excited to speculate that they had found a pregnant dinosaur and that maybe some dinosaurs gave birth to live young, like mammals, rather than laying eggs that hatched. After more research they thought that the skeletons were from a fully-grown species of small dinosaur that had been eaten by the *Coelophysis*. The latest thinking is that the small skeletons were from young *Coelophysis* that were eaten by the adults in a time of drought.

△ *Coprolites reveal the remains of what dinosaurs have eaten.*

DID YOU KNOW? Studying teeth can help uncover an animal's diet.

25

DINOSAUR COMMUNITIES

Some types of dinosaurs may have lived in communities, or herds, helping each other to stay alive, raise their young, and find food. They may have even traveled together, using migration to find more food.

Dinosaur families

One of the most important types of communities is the family. Dinosaur families were different, depending on the species. Some dinosaurs may have even had the same mate for life. Mother dinosaurs laid eggs. Sometimes the mother tended them and sometimes hid them and left them to survive on their own. Each style of parenting was designed to ensure the survival of the species.

For the mothers who tended their eggs, the advantage was that they could protect their young by fending off scavengers. When the young hatched, an attentive parent could keep them safe until they were able to take care of themselves.

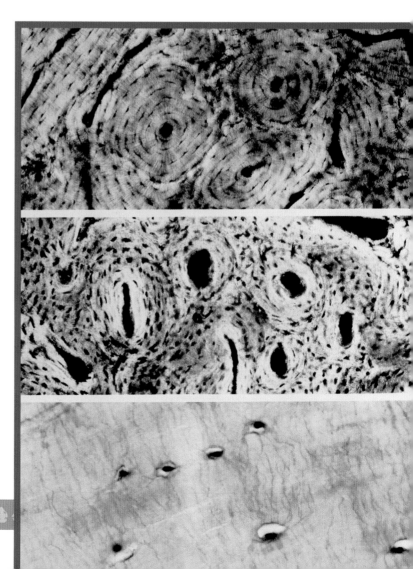

▷ *Microscope slides allow paleontologists to examine dinosaur remains very closely.*

Nests

Since there are many types of dinosaurs, we have to assume that there were many styles of nests, and patterns of egg laying. Most of them probably involved creating a bowl-like depression or tunnel in soil or vegetation. The number of eggs laid could be as few as one or as many as twenty or more. They might be arranged in a close circle, or dispersed and hidden from predators. They could be as small as an apple or as big as a melon.

Hatching

Sauropod females laid up to 30 eggs in a short span of time, usually at the edge of wooded areas. If they all hatched at once, there would be too many babies for a predator to gobble up at once and more of them would survive than if they emerged one by one. So hatchlings may have made sounds while breaking out of their eggs that the other babies could hear through their shells. Once out of their eggs, they headed straight for the cover of the forest.

Paleontology Challenge

When paleontologists study fossil eggs, they can have difficulty figuring out the original placement of the eggs. This is because if they were laid in a mound of vegetation, the plant material would have decomposed over time and the eggs would have rolled out of their original position. Also, geological changes, such as erosion and the depositing of sediment, would alter the placement. Even animals digging up the nest would have an effect.

△ *So far paleontologists have not found a dinosaur that reproduced without laying eggs. These eggs are from a* Tyrannosaurus rex.

Group living

Like animals of today, dinosaurs interacted with the other animals around them in order to eat, mate, and protect themselves. Many of the animals they interacted with were dinosaurs. Others were the ancestors of today's frogs, turtles, crocodiles, and mammals. For millions of years, they coexisted, maintaining a balance of nature.

When paleontologists find groups of dinosaur fossils together, it can be difficult to piece together their story. For instance they may have died at the same time, perhaps while migrating together or gathering at a favorite feeding stop or water source. Or they may have died individually over a number of years in the same place. Even if they died together, it still cannot be assumed that they always traveled in each other's company. They may have been driven to that spot by a predator or flood waters. Therefore much of what we believe about dinosaur behavior has been worked out from what we know about other animals.

Fantasy or Fact?

Some fossilized baby dinosaurs have been found, still in the nest, with worn teeth. This has been used as evidence that some dinosaur parents brought food to the young in the nest. Further research has revealed a surprise. Even dinosaur fossils that are found still in the egg, unhatched, have worn teeth. Paleontologists believe that baby dinosaurs may grind their teeth, even before they are born. But, this does not mean that dinosaurs did not feed their babies in the nest. It just means that we cannot be sure of it just from the evidence of their worn teeth.

▽ *Some types of dinosaurs may have traveled together in herds.*

A need to feed

The way animals behave often depends on how they look for food. We assume that dinosaurs used some pack teamwork when hunting. Dinosaurs working together may have been able to coordinate their efforts to bring down larger animals for food. Teamwork would also be a great defense for prey animals, who might herd together in order to fend off danger and to protect young. Climate conditions might also motivate mass migrations of dinosaurs. Sometimes they were simply all following the natural landscape, perhaps the edge of a stream.

Mating

The need to find mates meant that dinosaurs had to get together. They probably had special displays and courtship activities. Males might have sometimes fought over the females.

▽ *Fossilized dinosaur tracks reveal that dinosaurs passed along the same paths.*

DID YOU KNOW? Dinosaur nests left space for adult dinosaurs to walk among the eggs.

ADAPTATIONS AND SPECIAL FEATURES

Like all living things, dinosaurs had the ability to adapt. This means that gradually, over many years and generations, dinosaurs' bodies changed in order to survive better in their surroundings. Those that could adapt had an advantage and more of their kind survived. These specialized features are called adaptations. Since there were dinosaurs on Earth for millions of years, they must have been very good at adapting. Adaptations varied between carnivores and herbivores, and between different species.

Defensive features

Some dinosaurs had very useful tails. For example sauropods had incredibly long tails that could be used like large whips to knock predators down. Tails also helped them to balance. The base of the tail was a strong anchor for the muscles that moved the back legs. Some dinosaurs used their tails like clubs, and the tails were shaped to make this work well. *Stegosaurus* even had spikes on the end of its tail.

▷ The **Euoplocephalus's** *tail was like a club for defense.*

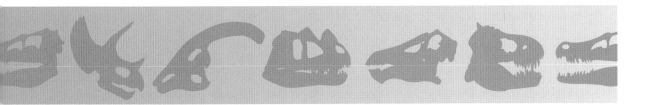

Spines and sails

Spikes or spines did not just show up on tails. *Kentrosaurus* had spines on its tail and also on its back and shoulders. *Amargasaurus* had spines running down its back that looked like sails. These may have been less for defense and more to keep them at the right temperature. They might have acted like solar panels to absorb heat, or they may have been used for display. They were very fragile, though, and had to be guarded from attack.

Horns and armor

In addition to spines and sails, dinosaurs developed other interesting adaptations, such as horns in the *Carnotaurus* and *Triceratops*. *Triceratops* and other related dinosaurs had neck frills that could serve as a protective shield during head-to-head combat. Neck frills could have had spines or spikes and may have also been used by males in display and competition.

Other dinosaurs developed skin-like plates of armor that protected more of their body. These dinosaurs were like armored tanks, and include *Gargoyleosaurus* and *Edmontonia*. *Stegosaurus* had plates too, but theirs stood upright and ran down the middle of their back.

▽ *The* Stegosaurus *had plates along its spine.*

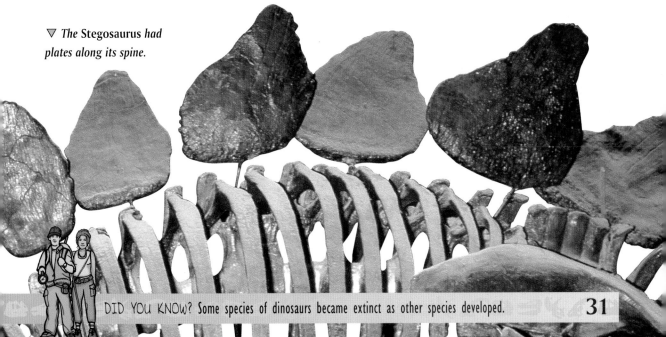

Adapting for survival

Teeth were designed to help eat specific foods. Plant eaters had teeth like shears or pegs that could strip leaves from stems or tear them from the plant. Some additional cutting and grinding might be needed before they swallowed, the teeth also had to be shaped just right for that. Meat eaters needed sharp teeth for seizing prey and cutting into meat. Their teeth were long, sharp, and serrated to pierce and tear.

Claws and beaks

Claws could also serve as eating utensils for dinosaurs. For instance *Deinonychus* and *Troodon* had sharp claws that could help catch a meal. Some dinosaurs had adaptations to their mouths, which made them like beaks or bills. In the ceratopsians a beak, much like the type that parrots have, was suited for the plant foods that they ate.

Fantasy or Fact?

Some people think that the Pachycephalosaurus used its thickened skull as a crash helmet for protection from attack, or as a weapon for ramming into other dinosaurs. But the bone of its skull was not especially strong, and the rest of the body was left unprotected. As far as ramming heads with another Pachycephalosaur, when the domes hit each other, they would slip too much. One thing scientists suggest is that the domed head might have been used to help them to identify each other. The domes would be like fingerprints, specific to each individual.

▷ *Some dinosaurs swallowed stones to help with digestion. The stones helped to grind up tough food in the dinosaur's stomach.*

Speed

There were many dinosaurs that were fast and agile despite their size. This was partly due to lightweight bones and strong muscles. The way they stood and moved also helped. Unlike crocodiles and lizards, who run with their legs splayed out to the sides, dinosaurs developed a posture in which their legs were held directly beneath their body. This was an efficient way of moving.

Mystery adaptations

Some dinosaurs had features whose purpose is unclear, like domed heads and crests. They may have been for temperature regulation, display, or creating sound. *Pachycephalosaurus* had a huge dome on its head that was up to 10 inches (25 centimeters) thick. *Hypacrosaurus* had a very high nose crest.

Paleontology Challenge

Only adult *Hypacrosaurs* have the high nose crests. Does this mean that the adults made different sounds than the young? Paleontologists have a difficult time reconstructing behavior from bones, but they can compare features with animals that we know well to come up with ideas.

▷ Triceratops *looks fierce, but it was a herbivore. Its frill and horns were probably adaptations for defense.*

TRACKS

Some dinosaurs walked on four legs, while some sprinted along on two. They traveled alone and they traveled in herds. Some traveled to escape danger, and others were on a steady path of migration, following food supplies and favorable weather. Their tracks are exciting to study because they tell us about living, moving, active dinosaurs.

EYEWITNESS

"...for bones are ever symbolical of death; but the footprints are those of creatures in the full tide of life."

Richard Swann Lull who lived from 1867 to 1957, one-time head of Yale University's Peabody Museum

Forming tracks

How do fossil trackways form? When the dinosaurs were alive, they left footprints where they walked, just like when we step into mud or sand. The heaviest dinosaurs left the deepest imprints. The soil had to be soft enough for a print to be left. But then it had to be baked in the sun to harden before a layer of sediment covered the tracks. Conditions have to be just right for the track to be saved for millions of years.

▷ These tracks were made millions of years ago.

WHO WAS Pliny Moody?

A young boy named Pliny Moody found the first fossil footprints we know about. He found them when he was plowing his family field in Massachusetts in 1802. The prints looked like large bird tracks. At first, people thought the tracks must have been left by the raven from Noah's Ark!

Finding tracks

"Dinosaur Freeway" is the name given to an area along the Rocky Mountains, from Boulder, Colorado to New Mexico, where there are billions of dinosaur footprints. In 1877 a teacher named Arthur Lakes discovered fossils of *Stegosaurus* and *Brontosaurus* in the Colorado sandstone of this region. Since then there have been many additional discoveries, including the Dinosaur Freeway.

A shallow ocean used to cover the area between the Rockies and the Midwest. Dinosaurs walked along the shoreline, leaving their footprints just like a child walking barefoot along a sandy beach.

▷ *Rich McCrea is a paleontologist who specializes in dinosaur tracks.*

Learning from tracks

Because tracks can teach us more about
dinosaurs, some people focus their studies on
them. The study of tracks is called ichnology, and
it is becoming a popular branch of paleontology.
Ichnologists can tell a lot more from tracks than
just the shape of a dinosaur's feet. Tracks give
clues about a dinosaur's posture, weight, speed,
way of moving, and adaptations. The size and
shape of the feet can help scientists to guess
about the dinosaur's other features. They can
even show if a dinosaur limped. Sometimes
tracks can even show more than feet. In some
places the path of a dragging tail can also be
marked on the ground.

Herd movements

We know that some dinosaurs traveled in herds
because of the trackways that have been found.
They may even have migrated, like birds flying
south for the winter. Ichnologists are interested
in things like whether the tracks seem to show
a steady movement in one direction, such as in
a migration. A collection of tracks that seem to
have no special order might mean it was a
gathering spot. By studying the tracks carefully,
ichnologists can decide whether one kind of
dinosaur gathered there or several.

▽ *What do you think these tracks
can tell us about their maker?*

Paleontology Challenge

Some *Brontosaur* tracks were found of only the front feet. This find made some people think that those dinosaurs could swim and that the tracks were made as the front legs pushed off from the sediment under the water. But paleontologist Martin Lockley suggests another possibility. Since those dinosaurs carried more of their weight on the front legs, the footprints from them were deeper and created a more lasting impression.

The size of the track can show the age of the dinosaur, which might indicate adults traveling with younger dinosaurs. Widely spaced tracks could show that the dinosaurs were running. What can be a challenge is trying to decide whether the tracks were all made on the same occasion or whether they accumulated over days or even a longer period of time.

In Texas, at Davenport Ranch near Glen Rose, sauropod tracks were found. At least 23 sauropods ran over muddy ground at a rate of over 6 feet (2 meters) per second. When paleontologists looked closely they noticed that small sauropod tracks overlapped the large tracks. From observing this they knew that the young sauropods were traveling in the back of the herd, either for protection or because they lagged behind.

▷ *These tracks are being studied to learn about the behavior of dinosaurs.*

PUTTING IT ALL TOGETHER

Finding fossils or tracks is just the first step in learning about dinosaurs. In the laboratory or museum, fossils need to be cleaned. Dental drills, artist's tools, and sometimes chemicals are used to dissolve away surrounding rock. Jackets with foam linings are made to store them. For display pieces, a supporting metal framework is designed that protects the display from falling while maintaining realistic poses and correct bone positions. Broken bones are fixed and distorted fossils reshaped.

▽ *This scientist is preparing a fossil for display in a museum.*

Analyzing fossils

Computers can be used to produce life-like images of what the dinosaur may have looked like, and they can even be animated. It is a huge leap from a skeleton framework to an image of a creature with muscles, textured skin, facial features, and perhaps feathers, or claws, or pointed spiny protrusions. But paleo-artists specialize in combining art with paleontology. They take everything they can learn about dinosaur science and create an image of a creature that no human has ever seen alive. Experts in biomechanics help animators to bring motion to those images, using the same technology that is used in movie special effects.

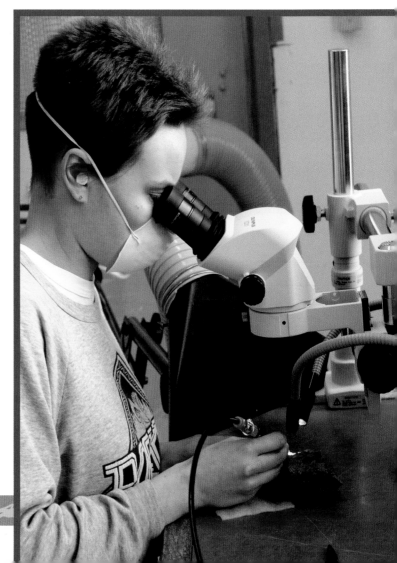

△ *You don't have to be a paleontologist to find a dinosaur.*

Amateur finds

The science of paleontology is exciting because new discoveries are being made all the time. People who find the subject fascinating can do their part to contribute to the knowledge. In 1995 a 14-year-old named Wes Linster turned over a stone when he was out on a fossil dig with his family near Glacier National Park in Montana. He saw a jaw with teeth. He had discovered a new dinosaur, and nicknamed it Bambi, because of its small size and gentle appearance. Further digging uncovered 95 percent of the skeleton. Sharp claws indicated that this was a predatory dinosaur quite different than its namesake. It was officially named *Bambiraptor feinbergi*.

Fossil collectors have a responsibility to dig only where they have permission and to share what they find for those who want to learn more about dinosaurs. Each fossil piece helps us to complete story of amazing creatures who preceded us on Earth.

The extinction mystery

There is a lot of speculation about why dinosaurs became extinct. There are many theories. One theory is that the rise of mammals caused the dinosaurs to die out. Carnivorous mammals may have eaten the eggs and young of the dinosaurs. Though an interesting theory, many have pointed out that mammals and dinosaurs managed to co-exist for a long time and so it is far-fetched to think that the mammals suddenly took over. Also, the biggest surge in mammal development came after the dinosaurs were gone.

Deadly volcanoes?

Another theory is that massive lava eruptions were the cause. Geologists can document these by studying submerged mountain ranges and layers of earth formed by lava. Geologists believe that there was a lot of volcanic activity at about the time that the dinosaurs disappeared. The lava and ash alone would have killed many dinosaurs. The gases that were released would have caused acid rain. Volcanic smog would have prevented sunshine from reaching plants, meaning that plants could not survive. Any plant eaters who lived through the volcanic eruptions would have run out of food to eat when the plants died. With the end of the herbivores would come the fall of the carnivores.

▷ *A volcanic eruption would have to have been huge to cause the extinction of the dinosaurs.*

Meteor!

A third theory is that a huge meteor, perhaps 6 miles (nearly 10 kilometers) wide, may have zipped through the sky at 150,000 miles (240,400 kilometers) per hour, crashing into the Earth near the shoreline of the Gulf of Mexico. The impact would have created a huge explosion, with earthquakes and tsunami waves in the ocean. Like in the volcano theory, the atmosphere would have been clouded with debris that would wreck the climate. Fires would have spread on the ground. Geologists have evidence for this in the way rocks have formed. They have also found soot from prehistoric fires and evidence of molten rock blasted from a huge crater beneath the Yucatan Peninsula in Mexico. The crater formed at about the same time that the dinosaurs disappeared.

△ *Geologists know that many meteors have struck the Earth. Did one cause the extinction of the dinosaurs?*

What's the answer?

There is still not agreement as to which theory is correct. It is difficult to decide between the volcano and the meteor theory since either event would produce similar atmospheric and geological results. Many scientists believe that the extinction of the dinosaurs was a combination of perhaps several of these circumstances.

PALEONTOLOGY TODAY

Paleontology is an exciting area of study today. There is a lot of public support for further study of fossils, and many museums specialize in exhibits that educate people about dinosaurs. There are many places that allow visitors to see excavated fossils, fossils that are still embedded in stone, and people working to gather and preserve pieces of the fossil record.

EYEWITNESS

"Upon my return home, the 'museum bug' had been firmly implanted, for immediately collections of fossil shells, rocks, birds' eggs, and insects were started ... the idea of following museum work as a life profession was implanted, an idea that never deserted me."

Charles Whitney Gilmore, 1874–1945, on the effect of a trip to the Carnegie Museum when he was six. He later worked there.

Technological advances make it possible to learn a lot from the smallest finds. Medical science, for instance, is where paleontologists turn for information about anatomy, biomechanics, disease, and genetics. It is also the source of high-tech equipment that takes observation beyond what can be plainly seen with our eyes.

There are many unanswered questions in the study of dinosaurs and many species yet to be discovered. Paleontologists divide on issues of extinction, behavior, and reproduction. They debate the classification of dinosaurs and their relationship to birds. There is plenty of room for new theories and discoveries.

▷ *Dinosaurs can be fascinating and fun.*

▷ *Many paleontologists are also teachers who pass along their love of dinosaurs to students.*

Careers in paleontology

For many people the study of dinosaurs is a hobby. Some of them decide to go on to become paleontologists. But how do you get started? It is important to read as much as you can about dinosaurs and science. There are also places that offer opportunities to dig with paleontologists.

Know your stuff

Paleontologists need to know a lot about science, especially biology and geology. Biology is the study of living plants and animals. Geology is a science that focuses on physical features of Earth. This includes rock formations and volcanoes, as well as the forces acting on them, for example, erosion. Math and writing skills are also needed. Because there is so much to learn, paleontologists must go to college and receive a degree and then continue their studies in paleontology at the masters and doctorate level.

DID YOU KNOW? Many important fossil discoveries have been made by children and students. **43**

Geologic time is measured as far back as about 4 billion years ago, which is the age of the oldest known rocks on Earth. It describes the history of Earth, based on the order of layers of rocks. Since fossils are often found in rocks, their position in the layers can help scientists learn when they were made. Geologic time is divided into sections called eons, which are subdivided into eras, periods, and epochs. We are currently in the Phanerozoic Eon, the Cenozoic Era, the Quaternary Period, and the Holocene Epoch.

PRECAMBRIAN ERA
4 billion–570 million years ago

The first life on Earth developed during this time. Most life forms were tiny and often had only a single cell. None lived on land. More complex creatures, such as dinosaurs, developed much later.

PALEOZOIC ERA
570 million–245 million years ago

During this period, there was an explosion in life on Earth. Plants and animals began to appear on land. Many different species developed, and life forms became more complex.

545 million years ago

The first primitive fish appeared.

417–249 million years ago

During this period, many species of insects developed. They were the first creatures to be able to fly.

At the end of the Paleozoic Era there was a mass extinction. More than half of the species on Earth died out, including 95 percent of all marine plants and animals.

MESOZOIC ERA
245 million–65 million years ago

Triassic Period
245 million–208 million years ago

At this time, all the Earth's continents were grouped together in a huge land mass called "Pangaea." The climate was mostly warm and dry, and there was not much volcanic activity. Life on Earth began to recover from the recent mass extinction, and many new animals appeared, including the first dinosaurs. Many of them walked on two legs and were fairly small, compared with the dinosaurs of later periods. Toward the end of the Triassic period, ancestors of the first mammals appeared. There was another mass extinction at the end of the Triassic, but it was smaller than the one at the end of the Paleozoic Era. The dinosaurs survived.

Jurassic Period
208 million–146 million years ago

Durind this period, Pangaea broke apart into two large land masses, Laurasia and Gondwanaland. Sea levels around the world rose, and by the end of the Jurassic many areas of land were covered in water. Many well-known dinosaurs lived during the Jurassic period, including *Allosaurus* and *Stegosaurus*. The first flying reptiles also appeared in this period, as well as the first true mammals.

Cretaceous Period
146 million–65 million years ago

During this period, Laurasia and Gondwanaland broke apart to form smaller continents. Earth's climate was also warmer than it had been before, and sea levels rose. Many famous dinosaurs, including *Brachiosaurus*, *Tyrannosaurus rex*, and *Triceratops*, lived in the Cretaceous Period. There were also flying reptiles, such as *Pteranodon*.

At the end of the Cretaceous Period, a mass extinction killed off all the dinosaurs. Many other types of animals and plants also became extinct at this time.

CENOZOIC ERA
65 million years ago–present

By the beginning of the Cenozoic Era, all dinosaurs were extinct.

At least 250,000 years ago

Homo sapiens, close ancestors of today's humans, first appeared.

TIMELINE OF PALEONTOLOGY

265

References to "dragon bones," which were probably dinosaur bones, found in China.

1452

Leonardo Da Vinci is born. He later studies fossils of shells and decides that they are the remains of sea animals. He was right—long ago the sea covered many areas that are now land.

1676

Robert Plot misidentifies a bone as being from an elephant and later thinks it is from a giant. It was probably from a *Megalosaurus*.

1769

George Cuvier, the "Father of Paleontology," is born in France. He later became famous for his study of fossils. He was one of the first people to think that volcanic eruptions and other events had caused the extinction of many species.

1787

The first dinosaur fossil documented in the United States is found. At that time the discoverers do not realize what it is.

1802

Pliny Moody finds first documented fossil footprints of dinosaurs. At the time, people think they were made by large birds.

1804–1806

The Lewis and Clark expedition discovers some dinosaur fossils on their voyage to the West coast.

1824

William Buckland studies a fossil of a jaw with sharp teeth. He realizes that it is unlike any fossil previously discovered and names it *Megalosaurus* (great lizard).

1841

Sir Richard Owen, an English scientist, suggested that creatures studied by Buckland and others belonged to a completely new group of reptiles.

1842

Owen names the new reptile group Dinosauria (terrible lizards). Its members later came to be known as dinosaurs.

1854

Models of *Iguanodon* and *Megalosaurus* are displayed in England.

1868

T. H. Huxley discovers that many dinosaurs had legs that were similar to birds'.

1887

H. G. Seeley divides dinosaurs into two major groups: Ornithischia and Saurischia.

late 1800s

Many dinosaur remains are found in North America, Europe, Asia, and Africa. In North America, Othniel C. Marsh and Edward D. Cope make many important discoveries.

1887

At Como Bluff in Wyoming, Othniel C. Marsh finds a huge number of dinosaur fossils, including *Stegosaurus* and *Camarasaurus*. Their discovery increases public interest in dinosaurs.

1889

First discovery of a horned dinosaur—a *Triceratops*.

1925

Dinosaur eggshells are found in the Gobi Desert by Roy Chapman Andrews and group he was leading.

1978

John Horner discovers the first nest of baby dinosaurs recorded in the world.

1990

Sue Hendrickson discovers the *Tyrannosaurus* skeleton later known as "Sue."

1995

Wes Linster discovers *Bambiraptor feinbergi*.

GLOSSARY

acid rain
rain that contains a lot of acidic chemicals

adapt
change to be able to do something better

anatomy
how the body is made up

animator
someone who uses technology to add motion to images to create animations

artifact
object from the past. Archaeologists often use the word "artifacts" to describe the objects they find that were made by people in past times.

biology
the scientific study of living things

biomechanics
the scientific study of how living things move

calcium
mineral that makes bones strong

cast
mold or imprint created by an object pressing down onto a surface

CAT scan
computerized axial tomography; a medical imaging technology

climate
weather conditions of a place or region during the year

continent
large unbroken mass of land such as North America or Asia

curator
person in charge of the care and administration of a museum collection

debris
remains of something that has been broken

display
perform to attract a mate

dorsal
along the spine

embryo
young animal in the early stages of development from a fertilized egg

excavation
uncover by digging

extinct
no longer in existence

generation
single step in a family tree

genetics
the study of characteristics inherited from previous generations

geology
the study of rocks and other land formations

habitat
natural home of a group of plants and animals

mammal
warm-blooded animal with fur or hair that gives birth to young who drink milk from their mothers

marine
having to do with the ocean

migration
to travel in search of a new place to live, often as part of a large herd or flock

mineral
substance found in Earth's surface

myth
tale about gods or other superhuman creatures. Ancient myths often set out to explain how the world began, why dramatic natural events (such as earthquakes) happen, and why people behave the way they do.

narwhal
species of whale with a long, pointed horn on the front of its head

nurturing
feeding or nourishing. Used to describe the way an adult looks after its young.

paleo-artist
artist who uses scientific information to create images of creatures that no one has ever seen alive

porous
having holes

predator
animal that hunts other animals for food

prey
animals that are hunted for food

replica
exact copy

reproduce
to come together to breed and
produce young

reptile
group of cold-blooded animals
including snakes, turtles, and lizards

resin
substance produced by trees that
hardens into yellow amber. Insects
are sometimes preserved in it.

scavengers
animals that feed on the dead bodies
of other animals or plants

sediment
fine soil and gravel that is carried
in water

serrated
sharply grooved edge, like the blade
on a saw, usually used for cutting
or tearing

sonar
sending sound waves out and
measuring their return as a means of
picturing hidden objects the waves
have bounced off

species
name used to classify a group of
animals who can breed with
each other

stagnant
still water without inflow of
fresh water

stride
length of a step when walking

tsunami
huge wave caused by an earthquake,
volcanic eruption, or a collapse

FURTHER READING AND FIELD TRIPS

Further Reading
Dixon, Dougal. *The Search for Dinosaurs*. Florida: Steck-Vaughn, 2000.

Holmes, Thom. *Great Dinosaur Expeditions and Discoveries*. New Jersey: Enslow Publishers, 2003.

Lessem, Don. *Armored Dinosaurs*. Minneapolis: Lerner Publications, 2004.

Field Trips
American Museum of Natural History in New York, New York.

Dinosaur National Monument in Dinosaur, Colorado.

Dinosaur Provincial Park in Patricia, Alberta, Canada.

Dinosaur Valley State Park in Glen Rose, Texas.

Field Museum of Natural History in Chicago, Illinois.

Peabody Museum of Natural History/Yale University in New Haven, Connecticut.